This book is dedicated to:

My first wife, Pam, the mother of my daughters, Heather and
Stephanie. Without her, I
would not have the blessings of our daughters.

To my daughters, Heather and Stephanie, whom I love very much.
I am so proud of them
and their walks with God.

To my wife, Deidra, who has given me a much-needed
perspective on my walk with the
Lord Jesus Christ. Without Deidra, this book would not be alive.

Finally, to my Mom and Dad (Ann and Bill), who have supported
me my entire life.

Thank you Jesus for being the King of Kings and the Lord of
Lords.
Blessings to all who read "Building Godly Men."

Kingdom Bound Men Foundation
560 County Route 64

Elmira NY 14903

607-738-4060

Table of Contents

Chapter

1

The Cry for a Kingdom Man

When your feet hit the floor in the morning, does the devil say, "Oh great! He's up." Or does the devil roll over and say, "Oh he's up, nothing to worry about here." We represent a King, THE KING OF KINGS AND LORD OF LORDS (Revelation 19:16). We became royalty when we accepted Jesus Christ into our hearts and our bodies are temples of the Holy Spirit. A Kingdom has one ruler. Our ruler and king is God. A king has subjects under his submission and a king rules by his word. God's word is the bible. *John 1:1 - In the beginning was the Word, and the Word was with God, and the Word was God. He was with God in the beginning. Through Him all things were made; without Him nothing was made that has been made. In Him was life, and that life was the light of all mankind. The light shines in the darkness, and the darkness has not overcome it.*

God has made institutions for his Kingdom, which include the family, the church and the civil Government. He provides guidelines in the bible for these three things. The primary component for a kingdom is the authority of the ruler. Satan first had to dethrone the ruler. When the serpent spoke to Eve to deceive her, he removed God's title of "YAHWEH" or "LORD" in all caps which means master and absolute ruler. When the serpent spoke to Eve he referred to The LORD GOD as just God, (Genesis 3:1-3). This little act changed the relationship they had with God. They were no longer intimate in fellowship with God, no longer walking and talking in the Garden with God.

When the sin occurred, the LORD GOD did not look for Eve, who ate of the fruit and was deceived. He called for Adam. Adam was ultimately responsible as head of the family. He stood by and let his wife be deceived and partook in the sin when he knew it was wrong and then blamed the woman! *Genesis 3:12 – Then the man said, "The Woman whom You gave to be with me, she gave me of the tree and I ate."* Remember also though, the woman shifted the blame as well. *Genesis 3:13 – and the LORD God said to the woman, "What is this you have done?" The woman said, "The serpent deceived me, and I ate."* But ultimately the man is the head of the woman and Adam should have said no. Adam heeded the voice of his wife instead of the voice of God. The result of this action is the loss of dominion of the earth.

Genesis 3:16-24 – To the woman He said: I will greatly multiply your sorrow and your conception; In pain you shall bring forth children; your desire shall be for your husband and he shall rule over you. Then to Adam He said, "Because you have heeded the voice of your wife, and have eaten from the tree of which I commanded you, saying, "You shall not eat of it: Cursed is the ground for your sake; In toil you shall eat of it all the days of your life. Both thorns and thistles it shall bring forth for you, and you shall eat the herb of the field. In the sweat of your face you shall eat bread till you return to the ground, for out of it you were taken; for dust you are, and dust you shall return"

SEPARATION FROM GOD

Kicked out of the Garden of Eden! Separation from God! Banned from daily communion with the LORD God! I wonder what that must have felt like. *Genesis 2:17 – but of the tree of the knowledge of good and evil you shall not eat, for in the day that you eat of it you shall surely die.* Not physical death, but spiritual death. We can liken it to the death of a parent. We have a connection to our creator, i.e. parent, and when our parent dies there is a loss of connection; the person who gave birth, raised and supported us is gone. We have great sadness at the loss. So when the serpent said in *Genesis 3:4-5 – You shall not surely die. For God knows that in the day you eat of it your eyes will be opened, and you will be like God, knowing good and evil.* The serpent did not lie. Their eyes were opened! Satan doesn't come at you with lies. He comes at you with truth and twists it. "Look at this beautiful tree! You won't die if you eat it!" He took away The LORD God's name and then he just left out the WHOLE truth! The death they experienced was spiritual death. Whenever we are in disobedience it pulls us further from our connection with the LORD God.

We Have Choices

There are only two answers to all of life's questions: What God says and what the world says. The Kingdom Man places himself under God's rulership and submits to the Lordship of Jesus Christ. *1 Corinthians 15:45 - So it is written: "The first man Adam became a living being"; the last Adam, (Jesus Christ) a life-giving spirit.*

Do you want order or chaos? The kingdom man learns the order of authority in the kingdom of God. The flesh man lives by everything he says and does. There is a lot of responsibility with being a Kingdom man. We have a spouse, children, career, community, church and any number of other things. A man who forgets what he is responsible for lives in chaos. The chaos created also results in division; division from God, division from spouse, distance from children, a failing career. Adam was left in charge of everything. Take care of the garden (Gen 2:15), name all the plants and animals (Gen 2:19-20).

Choose today! Maybe you don't want to have all this responsibility. Maybe you want to remain weak and powerless. OR maybe you want to be a true leader of your house. And maybe you want to know the authority we have in Jesus Christ. Our goal is to equip men to fully understand and implement the tools to reach their divine destiny in the Lord, which is how to be a man the bible way. (Kingdom Bound Man) *Joshua 24:15 - "But maybe you don't want to serve the LORD. You must choose for yourselves today. Today you must decide who you will serve. Will you serve the gods that your ancestors worshiped when they lived on the other side of the Euphrates River? Or will you serve the gods of the Amorites who lived in this land? You must choose for yourselves. But as for me and my family, we will serve the LORD."*

KINGDOM BOUND MEN FOUNDATION

It is time to get off the fence of indecision! The LORD God says in *Revelation 3:16 - GOD will vomit you who are lukewarm, out of HIS mouth, for you are neither hot or cold in your belief.* Choose well! Your choices change your life FOREVER! *Deuteronomy 30:15 & 19 – See I have set before you today life and good, death and evil . . . . . I call heaven and earth as witnesses today against you, that I have set before your life and death, blessing and cursing; therefore **choose life**, that both you and your descendants may live.* God tells you how to decide, CHOOSE LIFE! Or accept the consequences.

Are You Ready to meet God?

Obey the commandments of Christ

WE ARE TO BE RESPONSIBLE. ACCOUNTABLE FOR OURSELVES, OUR WIVES, AND OUR CHILDREN

Ecclesiastes 12:13-14 This is the last word. All has been said. Have fear of God and keep his laws; because this is right for every man. God will be judge of every work, with every secret thing, good or evil.

A man is an image bearer of God

Genesis 1:26 And God said, Let us make man in our image, like us: and let him have rule over the fish of the sea and over the birds of the air and over the cattle and over all the earth and over every living thing which goes flat on the earth.

Man and woman are equals

Galatians 3:28 There is no Jew or Greek, servant or free, male or female: because you are all one in Jesus Christ.

1Corinthians 11:7 For it is not right for a man to have his head covered, because he is the image and glory of God: but the woman is the glory of the man.

Think about what has been said so far. I have given an introduction to the world of the kingdom man. You have heard the overview of the kingdom man's authority. You have free choice; the LORD God will never force you to make a decision.

John 3:16 – *For God so loved the world that He gave His only begotten Son, that whosoever believes in Him should not perish but have everlasting life.* Unconditional love, love by choice; not based on feeling or chemistry. It just is! Agape love, God love.

Sinner's prayer

If you are ready to make that choice, you must feel it in your heart; a pulling within you. Below is a prayer to say, to make this first step, but feel free to pour out your heart to God in your own words.

"Heavenly Father, have mercy on me, a sinner. I believe in You and that Your word is true. I believe that Jesus Christ is the Son of the living God and that He died on the cross so that I may now have forgiveness for my sins and eternal life. I know that without you in my heart, my life is meaningless.

I believe in my heart that you, Lord God, raised Him from the dead. Please Jesus forgive me, for every sin I have ever committed or done in my heart, please Lord Jesus forgive me and come into my heart as my personal Lord and Savior today. I need you to be my Father and my friend.

I give you my life and ask you to take full control from this moment on. I pray this in the name of Jesus Christ."

A Man's Call to Greatness

Men long to be great!

How do we obtain greatness for God? How do we maximize our potential for the Glory of God and for the good of others? *1 Thessalonians 4:1-2 – Finally then brethren, we urge and exhort in the Lord Jesus that you should abound more and more, just as you received from us how you ought to walk and to please God; for you know what commandments we gave you through the Lord Jesus.* Even more important than being great, how do we do this and not take all the glory for ourselves? We are selfish as human beings. We start saying "Look at all I can do" instead of "Look at what God can do through me." *1 Corinthians 3:5-9 – Who then is Paul, and who is Apollos but ministers through whom you believed as the Lord gave to each one? I planted, Apollos watered, but God gave the increase. So then neither he who plants is anything, nor he who waters, but God who gives the increase. Now he who plants and he who waters are one, and each one will receive his own reward according to his own labor. For we are God's fellow workers; you are God's field, you are God's building.* The bible says in that verse, we have nothing to boast about, God gives the increase. We are the buildings, God is the contractor! He puts his Holy Spirit in us and starts working

on His plan. If we let God work through us, our building will be built on the Rock of the Lord Jesus and nothing will move us. See in *Matthew 7:24-27* and *Luke 6:47-49,* he is like a man building a house who dug deep and laid the foundation on the Rock. And when the flood rose, the stream beat vehemently against that house and could not shake it *for it was founded on the Rock.* And the next verse, but he who builds his house on the earth with no foundation when the waters rose and the stream vehemently beat against the house it immediately fell.

1Corinthians 15:58 – Therefore, my beloved brethren, be steadfast immovable, always abounding in the work of the Lord, knowing that your labor is not in vain in the Lord. What we do for the Lord means something and it gives a sense of purpose. Laboring for the Lord helps to give us understanding that we are here for a reason and not just drifting along wondering if we are doing the right thing.

1 Corinthians 10:31 – Therefore, whether you eat or drink, or whatever you do, do all to the glory of God. Human nature has not changed since the beginning of time and neither has God's word. He is our source of power for godly living by the Holy Spirit. Our motivation is love and our goal is to glorify God. Study the bible and the truth inside the cover will change your life from the inside out.

Some nameless religions teach that it is wrong to desire and lust, or that passion is a sin! Desire, lust and passion drive us toward our goal. YES, when it drives us toward a sinful goal it is wrong or prideful. When we put those emotions for the GOOD it is a different story. Be passionate for our God and what makes Him cry. Things like; reaching the lost, helping the less fortunate, loving His people and drawing them to Him. Here's a cliché, "What Would Jesus Do?" This was popular for some time, but the real question is, "What would YOU do for Jesus?" If you only had a certain amount of time to live OR if you knew when Jesus was returning, what would you do? Reach out to everyone? Help the poor? Feed the hungry? Tell all to repent the Kingdom of Heaven is at hand? This sounds a lot like John the Baptist as he prepared the way for a man whose sandals he was unworthy to carry, (*Matthew 3:3-11*). John the Baptist was preparing for his coming, and we should be preparing for His return. This is righteous desire, lust and passion!

Oh how many great men there are in the bible? Abraham (Abram); *Genesis 12:2 – I will make you a great nation; I will bless you And mark your name great And you will be a blessing. Genesis18:17-18 – And the Lord said, "Shall I hide from Abraham what I am doing, since Abraham shall surely become a great and mighty nation, and all the nations of the earth shall be blessed in him.* David; *2 Samuel 7:9 – And I have been with you wherever you have gone, and have cut off all your enemies from before you, and have made you a great name, like the name of the great men who are on the earth;* **John 14:12** *– Most assuredly I say to you, he who believes in Me, the works that I do he will do also; and greater works than these he will do, because I go to My Father. And whatever you ask in MY name, that I will do, that the Father may be glorified in the Son. If you ask anything in My name, I will do it.* The key to walking the path is still available today. When blessing comes for our work, our service, our ministry – what do we do? Stop and Rest. I am not saying we don't need to rest, even God rested. Keep going, keep working *Luke 9:62 – But Jesus said to him, "No one, having put his hand to the plow, and looking back, is fit for the Kingdom of God."* Don't stop and don't look back or we are backsliding. Give God the glory: *Isaiah 2:17 – The loftiness of man shall be bowed down, And the haughtiness of men shall be brought low; The LORD alone will be exalted in that day.* Do not allow yourself to be tempted when everything is amazing, remember to give credit where it is due. There will be days when we have to fight with everything we have to praise Him and days when praise comes easy. In those days of blessing do not forget whom it comes from! Don't be satisfied standing on the sidelines watching the game. Don't watch the parade go by when you can be in it. Don't be caught on the fence of indecision when Jesus returns. You will watch all the great men of God fly away and you will be stuck on the sidelines fighting for your life. Align yourself with God's word and God's kingdom. Make His agenda YOUR agenda!

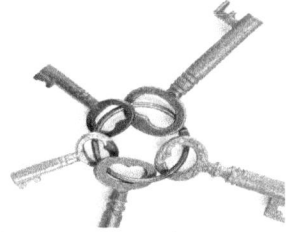

The Power of One Real Man

What kind of power do you have?

Judges 3:31 – **After him was Shamgar the son of Anath, who killed six hundred Philistines with an ox goad; and he also delivered Israel**

Shamgar was one of six minor judges God raised up to deliver Israel from the plunderers. (*Judges 2:16*) We should know some of the history of the Jewish nation if we read the bible. The children of Israel were constantly stepping out of God's protection and doing their own thing. And what would our loving God do? Save them! *Judges 2:11-18* – *Then the children of Israel did evil in the sight of the LORD, and served the Baals; and they forsook the LORD God of their fathers, who had brought them out of the land of Egypt; and they followed other gods from among the gods of the people who were all around them, and they bowed down to them; and they provoked the LORD to anger. They forsook the LORD and served Baal and the Ashtoreths. And the anger of the LORD was hot against Israel. So He delivered them into the hands of plunderers who despoiled them; and He sold them into the hands of their enemies all around, so that they could no longer stand before their enemies. Wherever they went out, the hand of the LORD was against them for calamity, as the LORD had said, and as the LORD had sworn to them. And they were greatly distressed. Nevertheless, the LORD raised up judges who delivered them out of the hand of those who plundered them. Yet they would not listen to their judges, but they played the harlot with other gods, and bowed down to them. They turned quickly from the way in which their fathers walked, in obeying the commandments of the LORD; they did not do so. And when the LORD raised up judges for them, the LORD was with the judge and delivered them out of the hand of their enemies all the days of the judge; for the LORD was moved to pity by their groaning because of those who oppressed them and harassed them.* Ok, I know this is all hindsight and I did not live in those times but why time after time did they fall away and get rescued? Even when they were left in the desert wandering around, God never let their shoes and clothes wear out or left them hungry.

Time after time, God rescued them from their own messes that they CHOSE to disobey and do. Our loving GOD said, "I can't leave them like this, no matter how much they anger me!" So He sent a great man. Shamgar killed 600, David killed thousands during a lifetime of battles (not counting facing one giant, by himself at age 14, named Goliath). God only needs one real man to fight the enemy. One real man who will stand up for righteousness. What if there is a whole army of righteous, kingdom bound men?

In the book of Judges, this was a time of chaos. Everyone was doing what was right in their own eyes. *Judges 21:25 – In those days there was no king in Israel; everyone did what was right in his own eyes.* It was dangerous. No rules. No guidelines. Israel was serving other gods, a.k.a the devil. Then here comes the super hero! Shamgar. A farmer with an assignment from God ~ kill the Philistines with your ox goad (an ox goad is a long wooden pole with a sharpened metal tip, used by farmers for driving animals).

What lessons can we learn from a "real man?" 1) Stop making excuses! Make the most of what you have. We all have talents. How do we use them? God gave us gifts to use for His purpose, as long as we are willing He will do the rest. 2) Advance one step at a time (the principal of multiplication). How did Shamgar kill 600 men? One at a time. Jesus promises in *John 14:12 we would do greater things than He.* Imagine, greater things than the Savior of the world?

What are you passionate about? Are you willing to commit and seek what you are passionate about? You are the one! It's your choice, take the red pill or the blue pill? Go on with the world as you know it or change your life forever! Choose wisely! Choose today whom you will serve, *Joshua 24:15 – And if it seems evil to you to serve the LORD, choose for yourselves this day whom you will serve, whether the gods which your fathers served that were on the other side of the River or the gods of the Amorites, in whose land you dwell. But as for me and my house, we will serve the LORD!* Don't be naïve and decide to not choose; that is also a choice! Whomever is not for the LORD is against Him. *1 Kings 18:21 – And Elijah came to all the people, and said, "How long will you falter between two opinions? If the LORD is god, follow Him, but if Baal, follow him." But the people answered him not a word. Matthew 6:24 – No one can serve two masters, for either he will hate the one and love the other or else he will be loyal to the one and despise the other.* Follow the LORD wholeheartedly or not at all. As my pastor often says, if you are going to hell, go all the way! Don't sit on the fence and waver between God and Satan. It says in *Revelation 3:16 – so then because you are lukewarm and neither cold nor hot, I will vomit you out of my mouth.* So let's refer to another "3:16" verse, *John 3:16 – for God so loved the world that He sent His only begotten Son, that whoever believes in him shall not perish but have everlasting life.* Which "3:16" sounds better?

Aligning Yourself For Impact

If a man is out of alignment with God, as a Kingdom man, it not only messes HIM up but everyone he has influence over. We are being watched by others and it doesn't take much for people to say, "See I told you he isn't really a Christian man." It starts at home. Men want their wives to respect them and submit to their authority as leader of the family. When we are not following God our wife cannot submit to us, ESPECIALLY if she is a Christian wife. Our closest friends who didn't say a word if we swore or had a beer with them, now they know the bible better than you and crucify you. So how exactly do we become men? How do we find our identity as male? How do we learn to be the bread winning, protective, supportive, Godly men we are meant to be? When do we become a man?

There are three stages of manhood: 1) **Sexual identity**. *Genesis 1:26-28 – Let Us make man in Our image, according to Our likeness; let them have dominion over the fish of the sea, over the birds of the air, and over the cattle, over all the earth and over every creeping thing that creeps on the earth. So God created man in His own image; in the image of God He created him; male and female He created them. Then God blessed them, and God said to them, be fruitful and multiply, fill the earth and subdue it have dominion over the fish of the sea, over the birds of the air, and over every living thing that moves on the earth.* **Gender identity** refers to a person's private sense of, and subjective experience of, their own gender. This is generally described as one's private sense of being a man or a woman, consisting primarily of the acceptance of membership into a category of people: male or female. [1] All societies have a set of gender categories that can serve as the basis of the formation of a social identity in relation to other members of society. In most societies, there is a basic division between gender attributes assigned to males and females. In all societies, however, some individuals do not identify with some (or all) of the aspects of gender that are assigned to their biological sex. When did you discover you were different from mom or your sister or your best girl friend? Did you take a bath with mom or play doctor? Until you "see" you are a boy, you will not differentiate between male and female. But do you see your destiny? You should be doing the Tim Allen grunt right now! God gave us dominion over the entire earth and everything on it! 2) **Boyhood.** *Luke 2:40 – And the Child (Jesus) grew and became strong in spirit, filled with wisdom; and the grace of God was upon Him.* *1 Corinthians 3:11 – When I was a child, I spoke as a child, I understood as a child, I thought as a child but when I became a man, I put away childish things.* The time we are children, a time of youth up to twenty years old. Immaturity, exploration but still dependent 3) **Manhood.** *Genesis 2:15 – Then the LORD God took the man and put him in the Garden of Eden to tend and keep it.* We work! Most men find their identity in their employment, which gives them a sense of purpose and responsibility.

The time of being an adult. Having the qualities of courage, vigor and determination (The Free Online Dictionary). What does God Say? Live out the principals and truths of His word. We have a responsibility. The Kingdom is not a democracy. God is the supreme ruler and under God is Jesus who makes intercession for us, under Jesus would be our Pastors and Leaders. Next would be the man who is over the woman and the children, and has dominion over the entire earth and everything on it. Do you recall what happened to Lucifer who tried to dethrone God? He was cast down along with one third of the angels in heaven. (*Isaiah 14:12-21*) We obviously cannot control every circumstance but we can control how we respond and handle our circumstances. God has the same issue. He cannot control us because we were given free will choice! He only has control in our circumstances if we choose to allow Him.

What happens? God gets blamed for everything! "God why did you let my child die?" "God why did you let my wife get into an accident?" "I asked you for that job God, where were you?" Am I preaching to the choir? Submit your life, submit to a Holy God, and raise your hands and surrender! Cry out and say, "LORD have your way in me and make my path straight!" Read His word and commit it to memory. NO! This doesn't mean life is perfect; nothing will be perfect until we walk the streets of gold in heaven. We can, however, start walking toward perfection. God will allow you to see the world differently. He will give you a new or a renewed purpose. When I finally submitted I discovered the Joy of the Lord. I stopped sitting on the sidelines and started playing the game.

Stand strong men! *1 Corinthians 16:13 – Watch, **stand** fast in the faith, be brave, be **strong**. Ephesians 6:13-16 – Therefore, take up the whole armor of God, that you may be able to withstand in the evil day, and having done all to stand, **Stand therefore**, having girded your waist with truth, having put on the breastplate of righteousness and having shod your feet with the preparation of the gospel of peace; above all, taking the shield of faith with which you will be able to quench all the fiery darts of the wicked one.* See, the Lord never said it would be easy. It is a constant battle but with the protection of God we can fight this battle and stand as men. It is a huge responsibility to be a man. You are the head; you have to answer for everything that happens in your "kingdom." So better to be on the right path and take the narrow door.

The components of being a man:

1) <u>Mentally</u> – Maturing into God's thinking. *1 Timothy 3:1-5 – This is a faithful saying: If a man desires the position of a Bishop (leader) he desires a good work. A Bishop (leader) must be blameless, the husband of one wife, temperate, sober-minded, of good behavior, hospitable, able to teach; not given to wine, not violent, not greedy for money but gentle, not quarrelsome, not covetous; one who rules his own house well, having his children in submission with all reverence* (for if a man does not know how to rule his own house, how will he take care of the church of God?)

2) Physically – *1 Corinthians 6:19-20* – *Or do you not know that your body is the temple of the Holy Spirit who is in you, whom you have from God, and you are not your own? For you were bought at a price; therefore glorify god in your body and in your spirit, which is God's.* Not only should we take care of the physical body (that we can touch) so we can carry on the mission of God but we are not to corrupt the body by giving in to sexual immorality.

3) Spiritually – *1 Timothy 3:16* – *And without controversy great is the mystery of godliness: God was manifested in the flesh, Justified in the Spirit, Seen by the angels, Preached among the gentiles, Believed on in the world, Received up in Glory.* We assume when we grow spiritually **WE** look better to others, but the truth is the more we grow spiritually the better **GOD** looks to others. In the same spirit John the Baptist said, *Christ must increase but I must decrease (John 3:30).* And **Romans 8:29** – *For whom He foreknew, He also predestined, to be conformed to the image of His son, that He might be the firstborn among many brethren.* We were predestined to be like Christ.

4) Socially – Fellowship with other believers and fellowship with Jesus. *Acts 2:42* – *And they continued steadfastly in the apostles doctrine and fellowship, in the breaking of bread and in prayers.* They read the word and socialized together. *1 Corinthians 1:9* – *God is faithful, by whom you were called into the fellowship of His Son, Jesus Christ our Lord. Jesus said in John 15:4* – *Abide in Me and I in you. As the branch cannot bear fruit of itself, unless it abides in the vine, neither can you, unless you abide in Me.*

Seven Attributes to Becoming a Man

1) Accept your masculinity – *Numbers 14:29* – *The carcasses of you who have complained against Me shall fall in this wilderness, all of you who were numbered, according to your entire number, from twenty years old and above.* Moses and Aaron were being told by

God they would never enter the Promised Land. Whatever happens, as a man, you are responsible.

2) <u>Speak with maturity</u> – *Hebrews 5:12* – *For though by this time you should be teachers, you need someone to teach you again the first principles of the oracles of God; and you have come to need milk and not solid food.* *1 Corinthians 14:20* – *Brethren, do not be children in understanding; however, in malice be babe, but in understanding be mature.* *Matthew 18:3* – *therefore whoever humbles himself as a child is the greatest in the kingdom of heaven.* With these three verses God is saying, mature and grow up but be like a child with your faith. Children believe without arrogance or self-exultation and willingly submit to God.

3) <u>Embrace responsibility</u> – *Genesis 2:15-17* – *Then the LORD God took the man and put him in the garden of Eden to tend and keep it. And the LORD God commanded the man, saying, "Of every tree of the garden you may freely eat; but of the tree of the knowledge of good and evil you shall not eat, for in the day that you eat of it you shall surely die."* We have a duty and responsibility as men; accept it and stand in authority.

4) <u>Function independently</u> – *Luke 2:48-50* - *So when they saw Him, they were amazed; and His mother said to Him, "son, why have You done this to us: Look, Your father and I have sought You anxiously." And He said to them, "Why did you seek Me: did you not know that I must be about My Fathers business?" But they did not understand the statement which He spoke to them.* During this time, Jesus was still a child and He disappeared from His parents. He was in the temple listening and asking questions of the teachers there. He was functioning independently from His parents to their dismay!

5) <u>Do not let your parents run your life</u> – *Genesis 2:23-24* – *And the man said, This is now bone of my bone and flesh of my flesh: let her name be Woman because she was taken out of Man. Therefore a man shall leave his father and mother and be joined to his wife and they shall become one flesh.* *Luke 18:29-30* – *So He said to them, "Assuredly, I say to you, there is no one who has left house or*

parents or brother or wife or children for the sake of the kingdom of God, who shall not receive many times more in this present time, and in the age to come eternal life.

Our parents should be honored (*Matthew 15:4*) but our parents have issues! Many times we are stuck in the past or in wrong teaching simply because our parents have so much control over our lives. How many people have had marriages ruined because of meddling parents?

6) <u>Lead the family</u> – Manhood does not mean you need to get married. Paul says in *1 Corinthians 7:8-9* – *But I say to the unmarried and to the widows: It is good for them if they remain even as I am (single); but if they cannot exercise self-control let them marry. For it is better to marry than to burn with passion. Teach your children **Proverbs 22:6** – Train up a child in the way he should go and when he is old he will not depart from it. Love your wife **Ephesians 5:25** Husbands love your wives, just as Christ loved the Church and gave Himself for her.* This kind of love is sacrificial, as you know Jesus died for us (His church).

7) <u>Be accountable</u> – No more excuses or pointing fingers and judging others! We will be accountable for our own actions and when we stand before a Holy God there will be no one to point fingers at, only our own selfishness. *Matthew 12:36 - And I say to you that in the day when they are judged, men will have to give an account of every foolish word they have said. Romans 14:10 - But you, why do you make yourself your brother's judge? or again, why have you no respect for your brother? Because we will all have to take our place before God as our judge. Romans 2:16 - In the day when God will be a judge of the secrets of men, as it says in the good news of which I am a preacher, through Jesus Christ. 1Corinthians 4:5 For this reason let there be no judging before the time, till the Lord comes, who will make clear the secret things of the dark, and the designs of the heart; and then will every man have his praise from God.*

Chapter 5

The Real Meaning of Headship

Mastering the Basics!

In this topic we need to have "unconscious competence," meaning we know that we know that we know and we don't think about it. Growing in Godliness means learning to live a life that honors God and follows the example of Christ. We must live in such a way that our lives will be a fragrant offering, pleasing to the Lord. *1Corinthians 11:1-3 – (Paul says) Imitate me, just as I also imitate Christ. Now I praise you, brethren, that you remember me in all things and keep the traditions just as I delivered them to you. But I want you to know that the head of every man is Christ, the head of woman is man and the head of Christ is God. Ephesians 5:1 – Therefore be imitators of God as dear children. And walk in love as Christ also has loved us and given Himself for us, an offering and a sacrifice to God for a sweet smelling aroma. Colossians 1:15-18 – He (Christ) is the image of the invisible God, the firstborn over all creation. For by Him all things were created that are in heaven and that are on earth, visible and invisible, whether thrones or dominions or principalities or powers. All things were created through Him and for Him. And He is before all things, and in Him all things consist. And **He is the head of the body, the church**, who is the beginning, the firstborn from the dead that in all things He may have the preeminence. Ephesians 1:22 – He (God) put all things under His feet, and gave Him to be head over all things to the church, which is His body, the fullness of Him who fills all in all.*

When Jesus left this earth for His heavenly Home, He commissioned the eleven disciples and gave man the authority to act in His Name. *Matthew 28:18-20 – All authority has been given to Me in heaven and on earth. Go therefore and make disciples of all the nations, baptizing them in the name of the Father and of the Son and of the Holy Spirit, teaching them to observe all things that I have commanded you; and lo, I am with you always, even to the end of the age. Amen.*

We have been given dominion and responsibility to fulfill our divine destiny. *Psalms 8:1-3* David sings a Psalm to the Lord telling Him how great He is and then in verses **4-8** David says, *What is man that You are mindful of him, And the son of man that You visit him? For You have made him a little lower than the angels, And You have crowned him with glory and honor. You have made him to have dominion over the works of Your hands; You have put all things under his feet, All sheep and oxen – Even the beasts of the field, The birds of the air, And the fish of the sea that pass through the paths of the seas.* Repeating the verses from *Genesis 1:26 God created man in His own likeness.* He is different from the animals and has dominion over the entire earth and everything on it. This dominion that was given to us makes us accountable for it. Our sinfulness caused a great flood. Our God promised not to flood the earth ever again and gave us a reminder every time we see a rainbow of His promise. We should be striving to live at our fullest potential and not merely dwelling at the lowest level. We have been placed just a little lower than angels! We are supernatural, spirit-filled beings! We have power; God given power!

God is the head of Christ and Christ is the head of the Church. We are the church. We are the bride of Christ. *2 Corinthians 11:2 – For I am jealous for you with godly jealousy. For I have betrothed you to one husband, that I may present you as a chaste virgin to Christ. Hosea 2:19-20 – I will betroth you to Me forever; Yes I will betroth you to Me In righteousness and justice, In loving kindness and mercy; and I will betroth you to me in faithfulness And you shall know the Lord.* God's covenant with us he likens to marriage vows, permanence, unfailing love, security, fair treatment and self-revelation. The church is a place for us to learn and grow and to fellowship with other believers. The church is not the "building" because if there were no people, there would be no church. We are the temple of the Holy Spirit, we are the church ~ living, breathing, walking around in the world and bringing our Christ everywhere we go. *1Corinthians 3:16 – Do you not know that you are the temple of God and* that the Spirit of God dwells in You? God's "building" made holy by the indwelling of His Spirit! **Romans 8:9** – *But you are not in the flesh but in the Spirit, if indeed the Spirit of God dwells in you. Now if anyone does not have the Spirit of Christ,* **he is not His. 1Corinthians 6:19-20** – *Or do you not know that your body is the temple of the Holy Spirit who is in you, whom you have from God, and you are not your own? For you were bought at a price; therefore glorify God in your body and in your spirit, which are God's.* The price that was paid, is Jesus Christ dying on the cross. He sacrificed all so we could have it all. Jesus blood was shed for us and be diligent to remember our bodies are not our own.

Man is the head of woman. *Ephesians 5:22-33* - *Wives submit to your husbands as to the Lord. For the husband is head of the wife, as also Christ is head of the church; and he is the Savior of the body. Therefore, just as the church is subject to Christ, so let the wives be to their own husbands in everything. Husbands love your wives, just as Christ also loved the church and gave Himself for her, that He might sanctify and cleanse her with the washing of water by the Word, that He might present her to Himself a glorious church, not having spot or wrinkle or any such thing, but that she should be holy and without blemish. So husbands ought to love their own wives as their own bodies; he who loves his wife loves himself. For no one ever hated his own flesh, but nourishes and cherishes it, just as the Lord does the church. For we are members of His body, of His flesh and of His bones. For this reason a man shall leave his father and mother and be joined to his wife, and the two will become one flesh. This is a great mystery, but I speak concerning Christ and the church. Nevertheless let each one of you in particular so love his own wife as himself and let the wife see that she respects her husband.* This is a sacrificial union. The instruction is clear that the husband is the head of the wife as the Lord, Who gave Himself unto death, is the head of the man. In return the wife submits to the husband's authority and respects him. Woman is designed to respond to her husband. Marriage is a unique relationship. The man is to "leave and cleave!" Leave the parents and cleave to his wife and she is to revere and honor her husband in the "fear" of the Lord. Fear of the Lord is not being afraid but it is Holy respect for Who He is.

This headship over the wife is not permission for him to misuse or abuse the authority man has been given. Man is not better than or more important than woman. Man has a huge responsibility in the marriage union and a there is a great need for responsible leadership under Christ. *1 Corinthians 7:4 – The wife does not have authority over her own body, but the husband does. And likewise the husband does not have authority over his own body but the wife does.* Mutual submission. Man and woman were meant to be one being and because of divine surgery, woman was created from man when the LORD God made Adam fall into a deep sleep and removed his rib. *Genesis 1:27 – So God created man in His own image; in the image of God he created him; male and female He created them. Genesis 2:21 – 24 – And the LORD God caused a deep sleep to fall on Adam, and he slept; and He took one of his ribs, and closed up the flesh in its place. Then the rib which the LORD God had taken from the man He made into a woman, and He brought her to the man. And Adam said: This is now bone of my bones and flesh of my flesh; she shall be called Woman, because she was taken out of man. Therefore a man shall leave his father and mother and be joined to his wife and they shall become one flesh.* So God took her out of Adam. Eve is bone of his bone, flesh of his flesh (*Genesis 2:23*). They are one sexually, spiritually and emotionally.

How to have Headship

Jesus commissioned man to go through the world and preach, sharing the gospel, but before man could do this he needed the power! *Acts 1:8 – But you shall receive power when the Holy Spirit has come upon you; and you shall be witnesses to Me in Jerusalem, and in all Judea and Samaria and to the end of the earth. All believers are given the promise of the Father. Luke 24:29 – But they constrained Him, saying, Abide with us, for it is toward evening, and the day is far spent. And He went in to stay with them.* Seek the baptism of the Holy Spirit, wait for it and then ask to be refilled daily and exercise your spiritual language.

Right now we are going to receive the Holy Spirit. If you have been baptized with the Holy Spirit already, ask for a fresh infilling.

KINGDOM BOUND MEN FOUNDATION

6

Foundation of Man: Dominions Roar

The lion in us

If a lion does not protect his domain, another lion will take what he has. A lion's roar can be heard for five miles. When is the last time you roared? Roaring is not complaining, moaning or grunting. *1 Peter 5:8 – Be sober, be vigilant; because your adversary the devil walks about like a roaring lion, seeking whom he may devour.* Be alert, the devil is crafty! It isn't just the devil you have to watch out for. Our flesh still has a hold on us, the world tries to entice and pull us back. When he is hunting, the lion doesn't jump on the first animal it comes across. The lion is lazy, it doesn't want to work hard, so it works smarter. The lion will watch a herd and find the gazelle that is slower than the rest or a baby who has wandered too far from its mama. So we need to protect our domain, be on the watch because the other job of the lion is to protect his harem of women and children!

✓ First foundational tip - **B**elieve, **O**bey and **W**orship Jesus! An acronym meaning "BOW" to Jesus. *Matthew 4:8-10 – Again the devil took Him up on an exceedingly high mountain, and showed Him all the kingdoms of the worlds and their glory. And he said to Him, "All these things I will give You if You will fall down and worship me." Then Jesus*

said to him, *"Away with you Satan! For it is written, You shall worship the LORD your god and Him only you shall serve."*

✓ Second foundational tip - Resist the devil. ***1 Peter 5:8***– *Be sober, be vigilant; because your adversary the devil walks about like a roaring lion, seeking whom he may devour.*

✓ Third foundational tip - Put on the armor of God. ***Ephesians 6:10-18*** *– Finally, my brethren, be strong in the Lord and in the power of His might. Put on the whole armor of God that you may be able to stand against the wiles of the devil. For we do not wrestle against flesh and blood, but against principalities, against powers, against the rulers of the darkness of this age, against spiritual hosts of wickedness in the heavenly places. Therefore take up the whole armor of God, that you may be able to withstand in the evil day, and having done all, to stand; stand therefore, having girded your waist with truth, having put on the breastplate of righteousness, and having shod your feet with the preparation of the gospel of peace; above all, taking the shield of faith with which you will be able to quench all the fiery darts of the wicked one. And take the helmet of salvation, and the sword of the Spirit, which is the word of God; praying always with all prayer and supplication in the Spirit, being watchful to this end with all perseverance and supplication for all the saints.*

✓ Fourth foundational tip – Believe ***Hebrews 11:6*** *– But without faith it is impossible to please Him, for he who comes to God must believe that He is, and that He is a rewarder of those who diligently seek Him.* Obey *1 John 3:24 – Now he who keeps His commandments abides in Him, and He in him. And by this we know that He abides in us, by the Spirit whom He has given us.* Worship ***John 4:23*** *– But the hour is coming, and now is, when the true worshipers will worship the Father in spirit and truth; for the Father is seeking such to worship Him.*

Realignment

Psalms 128 - *Blessed is everyone who fears the LORD, who walks in His ways. When you eat the labor of your hands, You shall be happy, and it shall be well with you. Your wife shall be like a fruitful vine in the very heart of your house, Your children like olive plants all around your table. Behold, thus shall the man be blessed who fears the LORD. The LORD bless you out of Zion, and may you see your children's children. Peace be upon Israel.* This is a generational blessing, "your children's children." *Psalms 119:1* – *Blessed are the undefiled in the way, who walk in the law of the LORD!*

When God made man He said let "US" make man in "OUR" image. Meaning the tri-unity of Father, Spirit and Son. Jesus was there since the beginning. In Genesis 1:26 God delegated the responsibility of managing his creation and everything on it. God still was king of his kingdom but allowed man to manage it. *Psalm 24:1* – *The earth is the LORD's, and all its fullness, the world and those who dwell therein.*

What is the devil's master plan? If he can get you down, defeated, thinking negatively, and feeling like you don't matter, he can stop you from entering into full authority and dominion. If you don't think you are GREAT, read what David said in *Psalm 8:3-6* again! *When I consider Your heavens, the work of Your fingers, the moon and the stars, which you have ordained, What is man that You are mindful of him, and the son of man that You visit him? For you have made him a little lower than the angels, and You have crowned him with glory and honor. You have made him to have dominion over the works of Your hands; You have put all things under his feet . . .* Halleluiah! Doesn't that give you a sense of power? The God who created you and the entire world knows you. All men should be roaring right now!

The devil does not want man to know this! What has happened since the 1970's? The women's liberation movement. Men have been slowly without much notice, losing dominion to women! Who is the leader in your family? I would say in at least 50% of marriages (actually most likely more) the woman calls the shots and may also make more money! So another thought, 50% of the marriages end in divorce in the United States of America today. Before women's lib, the divorce rate was around 20%. In the 1970's divorce skyrocketed and new laws came out for no fault divorce. Women were allowed to take dominion. Now first I have to say not all of it was bad, women got the right to vote and other privileges they did not previously have. Now watch as men stand down as the head of the household, women lost the right to stay home and take care of the house and the children and let the man bring home the bacon and work hard. Now women work hard! Most people do not have a clue how this change changed the world. It has caused a break down in society and men do not know their worth! Men do not take responsibility for their actions! How many fatherless children are in the world? CHILDREN NEED FATHERS! Women don't know how to grow a man into adulthood, into manhood!

God has a plan for YOU! *Jeremiah 29:11 – For I know the thoughts I have for you, says the LORD, thoughts of peace and not evil, to give you a future and a hope.* And THEN if we turn to the LORD: *Jeremiah 29:12-14 – then you will call upon Me and go pray to Me, and I will listen you. And you will seek Me and find Me, when you search for Me with all your heart. I will be found by you , says the LORD, and I will bring you back from your captivity; I will gather you from where I have driven you, says the LORD, and I will bring you to the place from which I cause you to be carried away captive.* He WILL save you and deliver you from your captivity! When my wife was feeling down and out a few years ago, the LORD gave her this scripture and it has been her favorite go to passage ever since.

WHERE ARE YOU IN YOUR CAPTIVITY? Rebellion? Idolatry? Deception? Corruption? Adultery? Laziness? Alcohol or drugs? What is your prison? *2 Corinthians 5:17 – therefore, if anyone is in Christ, he is a new creation; old things have passed away; behold, all things have become new.* Because of God's mercy and grace and the redemption by Christ's blood shed on the cross. The Messiah was crucified, dead and buried and then resurrected by the power of the Holy Spirit. Do you think our Savior wanted to go through this? He was blameless!

Matthew 26:42 & Mark 14:36 – Abba, Father, all things are possible for You. Take this cup away from me; nevertheless, not what I will, but what You will.

OBEDIENT UNTO DEATH.

Authority to Rule

David and Goliath

It only takes one man to rule. Goliath had an entire army behind him and David a boy 16 years of age, no armor with a sling and a stone. David was chosen by God to be the next king. *1 Samuel 16* Saul has been rejected by God as king and God sent Samuel the prophet to see Jesse the Bethlehemite. Jesse presented his seven sons but not one of them was the chosen one. Samuel said to Jesse *v.11* *"Are all the young men here?" Then he said, "There remains yet the youngest and there he is, tending the sheep." And Samuel said to Jesse, "Send and bring him. For we will not sit down till he comes here."* Samuel was told by the LORD to rise, for David was the one, and he anointed David with oil and from that moment, God was with David. David was a musician and was used to console King Saul with music and then became Saul's armor bearer.

1 Samuel 17 The Philistines had gathered together for battle against Israel. David's brothers were part of Israel's army. David at the word of his father Jesse, would take food to his brothers. During this time, Goliath, the Philistines "champion" was daring anyone to face him in battle. This had been going on for 40 days and nights. David heard the threats of the giant and said, *"so what does the man get who faces the giant? For who is this uncircumcised Philistine, that he should defy the armies of the living God?"(v.26)* David was taunted by his brothers and the army. Saul told him he is unable to go against the Philistine because he is just a youth. (v.33)

V. 38-39 Saul tried to fit David with his own armor, but it was too big. He couldn't walk. He took it off and went to find five smooth stones. – Goliath cursed David and threatened him and David said in return, *"You come at me with a sword, with a spear and with a javelin. But I come to you in the name of the LORD of hosts, the god of the armies of Israel, whom you have defied. This day the LORD will deliver you into my hand and I will strike you and take your head from you. And this day I will give the carcasses of the camp of the Philistines to the birds of the air and the wild beasts of the earth, that all the earth may know that there is a God in Israel.*

Everything we do, do it in Jesus' Name for God's glory. NEVER for our own glory. The GREAT men of the bible all had one thing in common! God's favor. *Psalm 30:1 – For His anger is but for a moment, His favor is for life; Weeping may endure for a night, But joy comes in the morning! Proverbs 12:2 – A good man obtains favor from the LORD, but a wicked man He will condemn.*

Jeremiah 26:19 – Did Hezekiah king of Judah and all Judah ever put him to death? Did he not fear the LORD and seek the LORD's favor? And the LORD relented concerning the doom which He had pronounced against them. But we are doing evil against them. Hezekiah prayed and repented for the entire nation of Jerusalem and God spared them even though they were doing evil things. *Acts 2:47 – Praising God and having favor with all the people. And the Lord added to the church daily those who were being saved.* We grow in the spirit by engaging in activities that consistently announce, embody and demonstrate the kingdom of God. We can never earn anything from God by flexing our spiritual muscles but we do gain favor by growing in the Lord and completing the task we have been commissioned to complete. It's like a race *2Timothy 4:7 – For I have fought the good fight, I have finished the race, I have kept the faith. 1Corinthians 9:24-27 – Do you not know that those who run in a race all run, but one receives the prize? Run in such a way that you may obtain it. And everyone who competes for the prize is temperate in all things. Now they do it to obtain a perishable crown. Therefore I run thus: not with uncertainty. Thus I fight: not as one who beats the air. But I discipline my body and bring it into subjection, lest, when I have preached to others, I myself should become disqualified.*

Here is the bottom line men: DO NOT LET YOUR GIANTS DETERMINE THE SIZE OF YOUR GOD! If you turn and run you have lost. If you "fight the good fight" God wins! How big is YOUR giant? In *Numbers 13:1 –* 14:45 The LORD spoke to Moses telling him to send out men to spy on the land of Canaan. This would assist them in attacking, know the enemy! Joshua and Caleb led a small group of men, one from each tribe in Israel. All of the men came back and reported how good the land was and even brought back some of the fruit. In *v. 27* they said the land truly flows with milk and honey. Even though it all was good, the men were afraid to take possession of the land God promised them. Come on, the LORD God says it's yours go possess it. I would think, "We got this; let's go!" And that is exactly what Caleb said in *V.30*. Except for Joshua, all the other men who went to spy on the land of Canaan were afraid and gave a bad report. *V. 28* The men are strong and the city is fortified. And *V.32-33* "The land devours its inhabitants and the men are of great stature" and "The men we saw were giants and we were like grasshoppers."

Israel once again missed out on the blessings of God. Caleb and Joshua exhibit true leader qualities and faith in God. Because of unbelief, ten of the spies saw walls they could not climb and men they could not beat, which carried back and made the entire nation fear and lose faith. Even though in *Numbers 14:29* God speaks to Moses telling him the carcasses of all who have complained against him will die in the wilderness (not enter the land of milk and honey, Canaan), in *V.30* he says specifically, "except for Caleb son of Jephunneh and Joshua the son of Nun." In *V. 24* The LORD God says, "But My servant Caleb, because he has a different spirit in him and has followed Me fully, I will bring into the land where he went and is descendants shall inherit it.

Face the Giants!

When your armor is on, the body is covered, protected. *Romans 13:12 – The night is far spent, the day is at hand. Therefore let us cast off the works of darkness, and let us put on the armor of light.* Jesus is the light. Put on Jesus. He is our spiritual armor, submit to his Lordship. He is the armor that is spoken of in *Ephesians 6:11*. The armor is not physical it is spiritual, meaning we can't touch it and we don't actually wear heavy armor. In *v. 12* it says we are not wrestle with flesh and blood but against principalities, power and the rulers of the darkness, spiritual hosts of wickedness. So you see Jesus is the light and the power. *V. 14-17* Our waistband is the truth of Jesus, our breast plate is His righteousness, walking with shoes of peace, peace in the midst of a storm; having a shield of faith, believing our God will protect us, walk with our head high carrying the helmet of our salvation and the sword of the spirit which is the Word of God.

God is waiting for you to do the supernatural. *2Peter 3:9 – The Lord is not slack concerning His promise, as some count slackness, but is longsuffering toward us, not willing that any should perish but that all should come to repentance.* Because of the Lord's delay in passing judgment, people think they have all the time in the world *V. 4* "Where is the promise of His coming?" People mistake the years of mercy and grace we have had for His weakness or that He is not coming. Present day humans didn't live in the days before Christ when God would spit on you and burn you to ashes if you sinned. If you disobeyed you were turned into a pillar of salt. Jesus brought a delay of punishment. Jesus is interceding for us. He sits at the right hand of the Father and says, "No Dad, I love them!" That is why He suffered for us. The Human side of God understands how stupid we can be and hangs on with hope that we will come to him and repent and not be lost to the enemy.

The book of Zechariah is filled with visions and prophecy. The first chapter in a nut shell, a call for repentance and restoration. *Zechariah 1:3 "Return to me, says the LORD of Hosts and I will return to you.* (The LORD of Hosts means He is the LORD of all of the armies of the universe) *V.6 My words and My statutes which I have commanded My servants the prophets. Did they not overtake your fathers?* God speaks through the prophets to align the church. *Isaiah 55:11 – So shall My Word be that goes forth from My mouth; It shall not return void, but it shall accomplish what I please, And it shall prosper in the thing for which I sent it.* His Word is Life and it spreads. Faith comes from hearing the Word. Part 2 of *V.6 Just as the LORD of Hosts determined to do to us, according to our ways and according to our deeds, so He has dealt with us. Lamentations 1:18 – The Lord is righteous for I rebelled against His commandment. Hear now all peoples and behold My sorrow. My virgins and young men have gone into captivity.* God is fair and just and full of integrity. Being righteous brings a person light and gladness.

The short paragraph above explains that: sin and rebellion = (equals) judgment and discipline. Acknowledge sin, confess it and receive God's forgiveness and mercy. The goal of judgment is restoration. V. 16 We are the Lord's house and He will return with mercy, we are his dwelling place.

1. Complete the task God has given us

2. Repent for not building the house of God

3. Restore and continually cleanse the temple

4. Bring the glory of God by renewing the ministry of the Holy Spirit

What will God ask you to do to show you the supernatural? Abraham was told to sacrifice his only son that he had waited years to receive. **Genesis 22:1-17** Abraham did not know the outcome, all he knew is he had to be faithful at all costs. At the last possible moment, **v. 10** Abraham stretched out his hand and took the knife to slay his son. **V. 11** an Angel of the LORD called to him and said do not lay your hand on the lad, for now I know you fear God and you have not withheld your only son from Me. V. 17 blessing I will bless you and multiplying I will multiply your descendants as the stars of the heaven and as the sand which is on the seashore and your descendants shall possess the gate of their enemies. Another generational blessing coming out of obedience.

We have boundaries!

1. Love God

2. Love others

Go do something. *Psalms 27:14 Wait on the LORD; Be of good courage, And He shall strengthen your heart; Wait, I say, on the LORD!* Waiting does not mean do nothing. Waiting on the Lord means to be about His business! *Isaiah 25:9 – And it will be said in that day: Behold, this is our God; We have waited for Him, and He will save us. This is the LORD; We have waited for Him: We will be glad and rejoice in His Salvation.* **Matthew 6:25-26** *– therefore I say to you, do not worry about your life, what you will eat or what you will drink; nor about your body, what you will put on. Is not life more than food and the body more than clothing? Look at the birds of the air, for they neither sow nor reap nor gather into barns; yet your heavenly Father feeds them. Are you not of more value than they?* Again, this does not say do nothing! It means God will take care of His people. When the Israelites were wandering in the desert, every morning there was manna on the doorstep and their shoes and clothes never wore out for forty years!! Stay under God's umbrella of protection. Don't do things you shouldn't to accomplish a task for God. For instance, hanging with the sinners in the places sinners go and preach to them. Love, Love, Love! Love the sinner and hate the sin. Tap into the power of the Holy Spirit and use faith. **Matthew 17:20** (Jesus said to his disciples who could not cast out a demon) *Because of your unbelief; for assuredly, I say to you, if you have faith as a mustard seed, you will say to this mountain, Move from here to there, and it will move; and nothing will be impossible for you.* How many of you know how big a mustard seed is? If your faith is this small you can still move a mountain, tap into that power!

Assessing Our Authority

My story in a nut shell. Lost awesome career, lost wife of 18 years, lost health (cancer). I had my wake up call. God blessed me and what did I do with it? God began working in me and on me by building a training company from the ground up, using my God-given skills as a trainer and teacher, completely healing me of cancer and bringing a faithful, Godly woman into my life. As I became more faithful to God, He began to bless me more and more financially. But a few years into my new marriage I became complacent and I began to slip into my old selfish ways and God gave me a wakeup call! He showed me how to protect my marriage and how to love unconditionally. It wasn't that I wasn't sincere in my relationship with God but I was not using God's authority. I did not know God as I should. I have my excuses, What is the value of our authority? We first need to understand dominion covenant. In **Genesis 1:28** we were given dominion and after the flood, God reaffirmed this dominion in **Genesis 9:1-5**. Jesus confirmed and sent us out to make disciples of all nations in **Matthew 28:18-20**.

Principles of operating within society: God gave men the authority to name, God brought every living thing to Adam and Adam named it. Naming gives us authority and influence. This separates the boys from the men. As a man, you get to name things and watch God bring them into being. It is your right and responsibility. Your name carries power and purpose. All will be according to God's plan, we can only name what God brings before us. Having a good name should be held above all, meaning you have integrity.   Your name means everything. God holds his name above everything! It is His authority! That is why when men came to salvation in the bible, God changed their names. They became new and no longer walked in their old ways. *Isaiah 45:4 – For Jacob My servant's sake, And Israel My elect, I have even called you by your name; I have named you, thought you have not known me.* *Proverbs 22:1 – A good name is to be chosen rather than great riches, Loving favor rather than silver and gold.* *Ecclesiastes 7:1- A good name is better than precious ointment.* *Proverbs 12:2 – A good man obtains favor from the LORD.* Get to know the Lord and obtain His favor, walk with integrity and love. Keep your name good and God will bring you things to name. True Success is fulfilling the reason why you were born and the reason why you were born again. For God's glory and not your own.

Chapter

8

Touching Heaven – Changing Earth

How do we touch heaven and change the earth? We have been learning how to touch heaven and now we will talk about our most important tool. Prayer. Prayer is our first priority in spiritual warfare. Thank God for our prayer warriors! *Romans 12:12 – Rejoicing in hope, patient in tribulation, <u>continuing steadfastly in prayer</u>. Acts 6:4 – but we will give ourselves continually to prayer and to the ministry of the word.* Pray especially before critical events *Luke 6:12 – Now it came to pass in those days that He went out to the mountain to pray, and continued all night in prayer to God.* Praying in all times for everything and everyone *Ephesians 6:18 – Praying always with all prayer and supplication in the spirit, being watchful to this end with all perseverance and supplication for all the saints.* We learned earlier about wearing the armor of God and being protected and prayer is how we engage in battle with the enemy. God's word is our chief weapon against Satan. Make intercession by praying in the Spirit or singing in the Spirit.

1) Pray in God's will - *1John 5:14-15 – Now this is the confidence that we have in Him, that if we ask anything according to His will, He hears us. And if we know that He hears us, whatever we ask, we know that we have the petitions that we have asked of Him.*

2) Prayer glorifies the Father - *John 14:13 – And whatever you ask in My name, that I will do, that the Father may be glorified in the Son.*

3) Prayer is based on God's character, ways and Word - *John 15:7* – *If you abide in Me, and My words abide in you, you will ask what you desire, and it shall be done for you.*

4) Pray with a clean heart - *James 5:16* – *Confess your trespasses to one another, and pray for one another, that you may be healed. The effective, fervent prayer of a righteous man avails much.*

5) Pray in faith - *James 1:6* – *But let him ask in faith, with no doubting for he who doubts is like a wave of the sea driven and tossed by the wind.*

6) Pray in Jesus' Name – *John 14:14* – *If you pray anything in My Name, I will do it.*

When Jesus died on the cross, He disarmed Satan. *Genesis 3:13* – *The LORD God said to the woman what is this she had done? The woman said the serpent deceived me, and I ate.* So in *v. 14-15* God said to the serpent *because you have done this, you are cursed more than all the cattle, and more than every beast of the field; On your belly you shall go, and you shall eat dust all the days of your life. And I will put enmity between you and the woman, and between your seed and her Seed. He shall bruise your head and you shall bruise His heel.* This is a promise that the Lord Jesus will trample the serpent or Satan at the cross. And *Romans 16:20* – *The God of peace will crush Satan under your feet shortly.* Which is the proclamation of the triumph of Christ over all evil fulfilling **Genesis 3:15**.

Colossians 2:13-15 – *and you, being dead in your trespasses and the uncircumcision of your flesh, He has made alive together with Him, having forgiven you all trespasses, having wiped out the handwriting of requirements that was against us, which was contrary to us. And He has taken it out of the way, having nailed it to the cross. Having disarmed principalities and powers, He made a public spectacle of them, triumphing over them in it.*

Satan still has power but he does not have authority unless you hand it over to him. He circles like a bird of prey, waiting for the right moment to strike. When we are weak, he comes in and starts talking trash in our ear. He waves a gun in our face with no bullets in the chamber, trying to scare and intimidate us. Kind of like Russian Roulette – will this be the time the bullet is fired? But God!

Colossians 1:13 - *He has delivered us from the power of darkness and conveyed us into the kingdom of the Son of His love in whom we have redemption through His blood, the forgiveness of sins.* We have been rescued from all of this. Being conveyed means to be deported or transferred from captured armies and populations from one country to another. So we have been transferred from darkness to light.

If Satan's gun has no bullets why do we have so many issues? Even though Satan lost, he is still fighting to bring others down with him into the pit of hell. He will try to make your life here on earth a living hell. We have all heard people say there is no hell, living on this earth is hell enough! The most effective tool we have against Satan is prayer and it is the most un-used tool in the shop. Why? Because we don't know how to use the tool and if we don't read the manual (the bible) how can we learn? The acronym for bible – Basic Instructions Before Leaving Earth. That sums it up!

What is prayer? Humbly, honestly, respectfully talking to God our Father. It is nothing more than how we would talk to our best friend or our parents. God wants to hear about your day, your fears, your joy, your accomplishments and not to mention, thanksgiving and praise for who God is and everything He does for us. Jesus instructed us how to pray in *Matthew 6:9-13 – Our Father in heaven, Hallowed be Your name. Your kingdom come, Your will be done on earth as it is in heaven. Give us this day our daily bread and forgive us our debts, as we forgive our debtors. And do not lead us into temptation, but deliver us from the evil one. For Yours is the kingdom and the power and the glory forever, Amen. John 14:12-14 – Most assuredly, I say to you, he who believes in Me, the works that I do he will do also; and greater works than these he will do, because I go to My Father. And whatever you ask in My name, that I will do, that the Father may be glorious in the Son. If you ask anything in My name, I will do it.* Sometimes we don't know what to pray or we don't pray as we should. In these times we need to exercise our faith and let the Holy Spirit direct us. *Romans 8:26 – Likewise the Spirit also helps in our weaknesses. For we do not know what we should pray for as we ought, but the Spirit Himself makes intercession for us with groaning's which cannot be uttered.* This means praying in the Spirit or in tongues. We need to be baptized by the Holy Spirit to receive the gift of tongues.

Know the LORD God. *Jeremiah 31:34* – *No more shall every man teach his neighbor and every man his brother, saying, Know the LORD, for they all shall know Me, from the least of them to the greatest of them, says the LORD. For I will forgive their iniquity, and their sin I will remember no more. John 6:69 – Also we have come to believe and know that You are the Christ, the Son of the living God.* Watch your behavior so others may know the LORD God. *2Timothy 2:24-25* – *And a servant of the Lord must not quarrel but be gentle to all, able to teach, patient, in humility correcting those who are in opposition, if God perhaps will great them repentance, so that they may know the truth.*

Listen to the LORD God. *Isaiah 55:2-3* – *Why do you spend money for what is not bread, And your wages for what does not satisfy?* <u>Listen carefully to Me</u>*, and eat what is good, and let your soul delight itself in abundance. Incline your ear, and come to Me. Hear, and your soul shall live; And I will make an everlasting covenant with you. The sure mercies of David.* He wants the best for us and it is free, yet we consistently will pay money for what is not the best for us. The LORD God says, "Listen carefully to Me; quiet your soul and hear Me."

Matthew 11:28-29 – *Come to Me, all you who labor and are heavy laden and I will give you rest. Take My yoke upon you and* <u>learn from Me</u>*, for I am gently and lowly in heart and you will find rest for your souls. Jeremiah 29:11-12 – For I know the thoughts that I think toward you, says the LORD, thoughts of peace and not of evil, to give you a future and a hope. Then you will call upon Me and go pray to Me and I will listen to you.*

Align with the LORD God. *Jeremiah 35:15* – *I have also sent to you all My servants the prophets, rising up early and sending them, saying, "Turn now everyone from his evil way, amend your doings and do not go after other gods to serve them; then you will dwell in the land which I have given you and your fathers." But you have not inclined your ear, nor obeyed Me. Isaiah 1:16-17 – Wash yourselves, make yourselves clean; Put away the evil of your doings from before My eyes, cease to do evil. Learn to do good; seek justice, Rebuke the oppressor; defend the fatherless, plead for the widow. Romans 12:9 – Let love be without hypocrisy. Abhor what is evil. Cling to what is good.*

You can hide but God knows your heart. *Luke 16:15* – *And He said to them, "You are those who justify yourselves before men, but God knows your hearts. For what is highly esteemed among men is an abomination in the sight of God.*

KINGDOM BOUND MEN FOUNDATION

But God is always ready to chat and give you another chance. *Isaiah 1:18-20* *– Come now and let us reason together, says the LORD, though your sins are like scarlet, they shall be as white as snow; Though they are red like crimson, they shall be as wool. If you are willing and obedient, you shall eat the good of the land; But if you refuse and rebel, you shall be devoured by the sword; For the mouth of the LORD has spoken.* Come now and let us reason together. God wants to debate and talk to you about whatever is going on. He is calling us today to reason with Him, though our sins are like scarlet, He can completely remove the stain. But this all comes through prayer, talking to our Father. He knows everything about us, He sees our hearts and He is always calling, pulling and tugging our heart.

Chapter

9

Claiming your Territory

God has equipped us with everything we need to exercise our authority, BUT God also gave us free will. We choose not to use our God-given authority and sit back wondering why we are not successful and happy and blessed. Are we like the Israelites who would not step into the Promise Land and wandered around in the desert for 40 years? I will explain our history according to the bible: We commit sin against God, we then are punished and left out in the wilderness to fend for ourselves, God calls us back because he loves us, we realize we are stupid and ask for forgiveness, God happily forgives us and we are back under his wings of protection. And it cycles back again. We have flesh that pulls us into sin, then rebellion against God and again and again He takes us back. Thank God He is faithful to forgive. How do we get out of this cycle?

RULES TO RECLAIMING OUR TERRITORY:

1) Leave the past behind! We cannot move forward if we hold onto the past mistakes, hurts, etc. *Joshua 1:1-3 - After the death of Moses the servant of the LORD, it came to pass that the LORD spoke to Joshua the son of Nun, Moses' assistant, saying: "Moses My servant is dead. Now therefore, arise, go over this Jordan, you and all this people, to the land which I am giving to them-the children of Israel. Every place that the sole of your foot will tread upon I have given you, as*

I said to Moses. Continuing through this first chapter of Joshua, God tells Joshua this is his "territory" and no man will be able to stand before him all the days of his life. Three times The LORD tells him to be strong and courageous and to do as the LORD commands and *Joshua 1:8 - this Book of the Law shall not depart from your mouth, but you shall meditate in it day and night that you may observe to do according to all that is written in it. For then you will make your way prosperous and then you will have good success.* So take your territory, do not look to the left or the right, meditate on His word day and night and you will be successful. If Joshua looked back at the past, he may have thought twice or second guessed God, which would have meant they stayed in captivity. We can't change what we have done in the past, we can't change the future, and we can only change or influence the present.

2) Seize your spiritual inheritance! Take part in your destiny! No matter what we are destined to have or be, it won't happen without action. We have divine privilege *Ephesians 1:3-6 – Blessed be the God and Father of our Lord Jesus Christ, who has blessed us with every spiritual blessing in the heavenly places in Christ, just as He chose us in Him before the foundation of the world, that we should be holy and without blame before Him in love, having predestined us to adoption as sons by Jesus Christ to Himself according to the good pleasure of His will, to the praise of the glory of His grace, by which He made us accepted in the Beloved.* We all have a calling. *Romans 8:28 – And we know that all things work together for good to those who love God, to those who are the called according to His purpose.* We walk not talk. *2 Corinthians 5:7 – For we walk by faith not by sight.* Use faith to pull down the blessings from heaven.

Hebrews 11:1 – Now faith is the substance of things hoped for the evidence of things not seen. Our faith is proof of what is unseen. The spiritual realm is more alive and active and more tangible than the chair you are sitting in; things you can see and touch. The world was made from nothing, by faith the worlds were created by His spoken word.

3) We are tied to God's word. Our faith is connected to our belief in God, which propels us to act. *Joshua 1:8-9 – This book of the law shall not depart from your mouth, but you shall meditate in it day and night that*

you may observe to do according to all that is written in it. For then you will make your way prosperous, and then you will have good success. Have I not commanded you? Be strong and of good courage; do not be afraid, nor be dismayed, for the LORD your God is with you wherever you go. **Psalm 1:1-3** *– Blessed is the man who walks not in the counsel of the ungodly, nor stands in the path of sinner, nor sits in the seat of the scornful; but his delight is in the law of the LORD, and in His law he meditates day and night. He shall be like a tree planted by the rivers of water that brings forth its fruit in its season, whose leaf also shall not wither; and whatever he does shall prosper.*

4)   Link all your decisions on the Word of God. When a man has a decision to make, where does he go? His best buddy (who is just as messed up as he is)? His wife (women are not supposed to lead the family)? His parents (depend on someone else's mistakes)? Every decision should go through God. I don't mean whether to buy toilet paper, "Oh God most Holy One, is this the right brand of toilet paper for me?" NO!!! Talk to Him, be in communion with Him, "Holy Spirit, what would you tell me about *this* situation?" Go to the Bible, ask for revelation from His Word. His word says in **Isaiah 55:8 – 11** - *For My thoughts are not your thoughts, Nor are your ways My ways," says the LORD. For as the heavens are higher than the earth, So are My ways higher than your ways, And My thoughts than your thoughts. For as the rain comes down, and the snow from heaven, And do not return there, but water the earth, and make it bring forth and bud, that it may give seed to the sower and bread to the eater. So shall My word be that goes forth from My mouth. It shall not return to Me void, but it shall accomplish what I please, and it shall prosper in the thing for which I sent it.* Think outside the box!   God knows all, sees all, His word has power to change. It brings light to darkness, truth to our errors, grace to cover our sin, power to convict men and cleanse our hearts from the stain of sin. Only HE, the LORD can lead you. Your friends will never give you more than they have, and will also pull you back, SELAH! Your wife is meant to support, respect, follow you - that is one reason our world is so messed up! Men are NOT leading and someone has to. Women are strong and are made to take up the slack.

They're multi-taskers. Your family, parents, siblings; chances are they are in the same "box" as you. Generation after generation (called a generational curse) tend to do the same thing, how can they help you lead the family? Like father like son or like mother like daughter His word is seed. Link our lives to His seed and we will bring forth a harvest, enlarging, expanding, God's power is limitless. From one seed we receive many. The law of seedtime and harvest. *Genesis 8:22 — While the earth remains, seedtime and harvest, cold and heat, winter and summer and day and night shall not cease.* The LORD will continue to multiply as long as the earth remains.

Something that holds us back from claiming our territory is a curse. A small part, just two verses, a little known man in the bible, Jabez. In my opinion, for God to want this in the bible means it is BIG! *1 Chronicles 4:9-10 — Now Jabez was more honorable than his brothers, and his mother called his name Jabez, saying, "because I bore him in pain." And Jabez called on the God of Israel saying, "Oh, that You would bless me indeed, and enlarge my territory, that Your hand would be with me, and that You would keep me from evil, that I may not cause pain!" So God granted him what he requested.* Jabez was cursed by his mother from birth, apparently he caused her great pain during childbirth. Can you imagine naming your child to curse him, but that is exactly what we do! My wife works at a prison, she sees names of inmates and constantly wonders if the parents wanted to send their child to prison. Names have great meaning and can bring blessing or cursing. What happened with great men in the bible? When God changed them, He changed their names. For instance, Abram and Abraham *Genesis 17:5 — No longer shall your name be called Abram, but your name shall be Abraham; for I have made you a father of many nations.* Abram means high father or Patriarch, the head of the family. Abraham means father of a multitude, which is a reminder of God's promise and covenant.

He will cause pain, is what Jabez name means. It says he was an honorable man and he was trying to overcome the curse of his mother's words. He called on the God of Israel; "Bless me LORD, increase my territory, let Your hand be with me and keep me from evil, I don't want to cause pain!" He is asking to be free from the curse of his mother, to expand, to enlarge his territory. *Proverbs 26:2 — so a curse without cause will not alight. Numbers 23:8 — How shall I curse whom God has not cursed: And how shall I denounce whom the LORD has not denounced?* Curses are subject to the LORD! *ONLY* the LORD can remove curses. We can fight and struggle to be honorable, respectable and do the right thing, but God . . . .

Isaiah 54:2 – Enlarge the place of your tent, and let them stretch out the curtains of your dwellings; Do not spare; lengthen your cords, and strengthen your stakes. Isaiah 33:20 – Look upon Zion, the city of our appointed feasts; your eyes will see Jerusalem, a quiet home, a tabernacle that will not be taken down; not one of its stakes will ever be removed, nor will any of its cords be broken.

To complete steps 1 through 4 in this chapter, continually pray the prayer of Jabez. Pray against generational curses of the past, pray against the curses that can skip generations and strike our children, pray against the curses we have created with our own sins. Become tied to the word of God, create good ground to plant the seeds of God, think outside the box and expand your territory.

Kingdom Man's Personal Life

The power of the trickle-down theory. Power, cursing, blessing, flows from the head down. Like the oil flowing down the beard of Aaron, WHATEVER we have flows from the head down. If a man who is head of the family is messed up, his family is messed up; take several messed up men and families and his church is messed up; the community is messed up because our men are messed up - which effects the whole world. We have more screwed up people in the world than ever before. God and the church formed the foundation of the United States of America. What is the root of united? Unity. Oneness. *Psalm 133:1-2 – Behold, how good and how pleasant it is for brethren to dwell together in unity. It is like the precious oil upon the head, running down on the beard, The beard of Aaron, running down on the edge of his garments.* And yet how divided the United States has become! We are not even allowed to teach about God in school anymore. Our men leave their wives and families. We have no honor or dignity; it is easier to quit than to stand up and fight. No one wants to go to war; bring our troops home! Does everyone forget we have peace and freedom because of war? Our God is a God of war and a God of Justice! The old testament of the bible was filled with war and blood, sacrifice and covenants.

It all starts with one man. It starts because of you. We used to fight for what we believe in and that starts with fear (honor and respect) of the Lord! Does anyone have fear that God will smite them? Of course not! We are in a time of peace and mercy and everyone is relaxed. Nothing to worry about, I have time to clean up my act before Jesus comes. *Psalm 128 – Blessed is everyone who fears the*

LORD, Who walks in His ways. When you eat the labor of your hands, you shall be happy and it shall be well with you. Your wife shall be like a fruitful vine in the very heart of your house, your children like olive plants all around your table. Behold, thus shall the man be blessed who fears the LORD. The LORD bless you out of Zion, and may you see the good of Jerusalem all the days of your life. Yes may you see your children's children. Peace be upon Israel! *Psalm 119:1* – Blessed are the undefiled in the way, who walk in the law of the LORD! *Ezekiel 19:10* – Your mother was like a vine in your bloodline, planted by the waters, fruitful and full of branches because of many waters. *Psalm 127:3* – Behold, children are a heritage from the LORD, the fruit of the womb is a reward. *Psalm 134* – Behold, bless the LORD, all you servants of the LORD, who by night stand in the house of the LORD! Lift up your hands in the sanctuary and bless the LORD. The LORD who made heaven and earth Bless you from Zion! *Job 42:16* – After this Job lived one hundred and forty years and saw his children and grandchildren for four generations.

So according to the previous scriptures this is a Kingdom Man:

1) Personally – fears the LORD

2) Family – wife is fruitful and children are lovely

3) Church – serves and worships "Zion"

4) Community – peace & prosperity be upon Israel

Blessing refers to favor from God. Blessing and goodness flow to you so He can get it through you. Nothing should stop with you! He doesn't bless and give us good gifts so we can say how good we are and how good God is to us. He wants us to have plenty so we can share with others. *Acts 20:35* – *I have shown you in every way, by laboring like this that you must support the weak. And remember the words of the Lord Jesus, that He said, "It is more blessed to give than receive." Luke 6:38* – *Give, and it will be given to you: good measure, pressed down, shaken together and running over will be put into your bosom. For with the same measure that you use, it will be measured back to you.*

Time to look inside and search the heart. Do we give out of our need or out of our abundance? Do we do nothing but expect everything from God? Are you expecting a harvest without planting a seed?

Luke 21:1-2 – He looked up and saw the rich putting their gifts into the treasury and He saw certain poor widow putting in two mites. He pointed out the widow had given much more than the rich person. The widow gave out of her need, giving all and expecting God to honor that and provide for her. The rich gave out of the abundance and cost them nothing but made them look real good.

Giving is sacrificial, whether it be your time, finances, talents, commitments, etc. *Luke 12:48 - . . . . For everyone to whom much is given, from him much will be required; and to whom much has been committed, of him they will ask the more.*

The book of Malachi is a message to the people about giving and sacrifice. We bring to the Lord our last fruits and not our best lamb. We bring our rotten fruit and not a tenth off the top. We don't give our best but expect God's favor. We do Him evil and then say God where are you? We weary him with our many words. We are cursed because we do not bring the whole tithe into the storehouse. In the end the Lord says to those who feared Him, He will remember them, they will be spared. Discern between the righteous and the wicked, one who serves God and one who does not. Behold, a day is coming, burning like an oven for the proud and the wicked, but those who fear the Lord the sun of righteousness will arise with healing on His wings!

God wants, desires, demands our best and that we take Him seriously. He desires that we fear, respect and honor Him. Don't give him our leftovers with time and service and then ask or expect His blessing.

Discipleship:

Matthew 16:24-25 – Then Jesus said to His disciples, If anyone desires to come after Me, let him deny himself and take up his cross, and follow me. For whoever desires to save his life will lose it, but whoever loses his life for My sake will find it. Jesus said to take up "your" cross. Not His cross, or your neighbor's cross, or your parent's cross. YOUR cross. We have to die to self. We are Jesus' apprentices and that means letting go of our own selfish desires and putting His desires first. My wife prays daily to hear God's heartbeat and to know what hurts His heart. We need to love like He did. *Luke 9:23 – If anyone desires to come after Me, let him deny himself and take up his cross daily and follow me. Romans 12:1-2 – I beseech you therefore, brethren, by the mercies of God, that you present your bodies a living sacrifice, holy, acceptable to God, which is your reasonable service. And do not be conformed to his world but be transformed by the renewing of your mind that you may prove what is that good and acceptable and perfect will of God.*

We are God Zombies!! We are the living dead!! Dying to our will, thoughts and desires while we are living for Gods will, thoughts and desires.

This is a daily act of sacrifice and not a thing we do once a week on Sunday. Take up our cross daily.

Kingdom Man's Family Life

Is your marriage a contract or a covenant? People break contracts every day. A covenant is about sacrifice. Every time a covenant was cut in the bible (before Jesus died and rose again) there was blood. An animal had to be sacrificed. The first blood covenant with Abraham in *Genesis 15:9-10* – *Bring Me a three year old heifer, a three year old female goat, a three year old ram, a turtledove and a young pigeon. Then he brought all these to Him and cut them in tow, down the middle and place each piece opposite the other; but he did not cute the birds in two. Genesis 15:17* – *And it came to pass, when the sun went down and it was dark, that behold, there appeared a smoking oven and a burning torch that passed between those pieces.* Only God passed between the two pieces because it was HIS covenant. This was the first covenant and promise to Abraham. There must be a blood sacrifice, the two parties to the covenant walk between the sacrificed animals and God is the sovereign administrator of the oath. So when we are married, under God, until death do we part, we are creating a covenant without the bloodshed. Jesus shed his blood for us once, for all, He is our blood sacrifice.

What would happen in the bible if anyone broke a covenant with God? See *Jeremiah 34:20* – *I will give them into the hand of their enemies and into the hand of those who seek their life. Their dead bodies shall be for meat for the birds of the heaven and the beasts of the earth.* The previous verses listed all the people who had passed between the sacrificed calf halves and broke the covenant. So it appears God takes covenants seriously! Now we all know we are in the period of grace and mercy, no one has been hit by lightning because of divorce or half of the world would be dead! We are at 50% divorce rate after all! But that does not mean that this is negotiable now. We have been hardened to the seriousness of the crime we commit when we break covenant. It is spiritually binding, no matter the outcome or the benefits.

Every covenant includes three fundamental elements:

1.   Transcendence – "God rules"

2.   Hierarchy – specific order of each components function

3.   Ethics – the rules of operation

   a.   Rules

   b.   Sanctions

   c.   Continuity

If your wife is to be like a vine, producing fruit and growing, she needs (a vine needs):

1.   Security, cling "leave and cleave" *Genesis 2:24*

2.   Climbs, trellis - able to expand and grow *Deut 20:6*

3.   Prune – ability to produce fruit

John 15:1-8 – Jesus is the true vine and The Father is the vine-dresser. Abide with Jesus and He will abide in you to bear much fruit. Without Jesus we can do nothing and as a branch of the true vine if we wither and do not bear fruit, the Father will prune us so we may bear fruit again. We need direct connection to the LORD God and His son to be healthy. And as our wives "cling" to us, as to the Lord, they will be able to grow and bear much fruit. The key is for US as the MAN to stay close to the true vine and as He nurtures us, we can nurture our wives. Our wives are made to be drawn to Jesus and there is nothing more attractive to a Christian woman than a man who is serving and under the control of her God. A Godly man should exhibit the characteristics of Jesus, temperate, kind, patient, loving, etc. You know the verses, the fruits of the Spirit! No one is perfect all the time except our Father in Heaven, but every day we are striving to be more like Him.

Ephesians 5:25 – *Husbands love your wives, just as Christ also loved the church and gave Himself for her.* Sacrifice

Ephesians 5:26 – *that He might sanctify and cleanse her with the washing of water by the word.* Marriage is Holy

Ephesians 5:27 – *that He might present her to Himself a glorious church, not having spot or wrinkle or any such thing, but that she should be holy and without blemish.* She is special and unique

Ephesians 5:28-29 – *So husbands ought to love their own wives as their own bodies; he who loves his wife loves himself. For no one ever hated his own flesh, but nourishes and cherishes it, just as the Lord does the church.* Jesus loves unconditionally, know her like you know yourself

Ephesians 5:30 – *For we are members of His body, of His flesh and of His bones. For this reason a man shall leave his father and mother and be joined to his wife and the two shall become one flesh.* We are "one" when we are married - as we are also one with Jesus.

Loving your wife is a choice not a feeling, as it is for her as well. So we must also choose to find out her needs. What we think she may want or need is not usually the case. For example: many wives are so happy when you bring them jewelry right? Not my wife, she hardly ever wears jewelry, so if I buy her jewelry, she appreciates the thought but what really makes her happy is just her car cleaned off and started in the morning! So understand her needs and she will think you are the most wonderful man in the universe.

Do you want your prayers to be hindered? If we do not live as kingdom bound men or husbands our prayers will be hindered. *1 Peter 3:7* – *Husbands, likewise, dwell with them with understanding, giving honor to the wife as to the weaker vessel, and as being heirs together of the grace of life, that your prayers may not be hindered.* Men should have a peaceful and humble spirit; be understanding of your wife. Honor her as an equal heir of salvation, so that your prayers will not be hindered.

Your wife will be like a grapevine and produce fruit. A virtuous wife is precious, she is pride of her husband and she is praised! *Read Proverbs 31*

Be intentional when complementing her and pray together often.

Your children will be like green olive plants around your table. The dinner table is a time to teach, listen, get to know and lead the family. *Psalm 128:3*

Stay close to Jesus, reject independence and develop a deeper relationship with Jesus. Your wife will be drawn to you and your children will seek your wisdom. Your wife will know when you aren't studying the Word because of how you treat her!

Kingdom Man's Church Life

*P*salm 128:5 – *The LORD bless you out of Zion, and may you see the good of Jerusalem all the days of your life.* The church is to prepare the believers to display God's glory, impact our culture, restore lives and advance the kingdom. Church is a community of believers using their gifts and talents to edify the body. The church body is not just one part, but many parts working together. Churches need men's ministry. Younger men should be taught by the more mature men to instruct, inspire, encourage, equip and to hold accountable. The word of God is not just something we need to know it is to be used. The word of God is a verb. It requires action and in all ways it can be applied to our lives. We need a spiritual father and to be one. A kingdom man should be a mentor, not something done once in a while but a way of life. Get involved and connected to your church.

What is a church? It is not the building, but the people inside the building. *Matthew 18:20 – For where two or three are gathered together in my name, I am there in the midst of them. 1 Corinthians 5:4 – In the name of our Lord Jesus Christ, when you are gathered together, along with my spirit, with the power of our Lord Jesus Christ. Acts 20:7 – Now on the first day of the week, when the disciples came together to break bread, Paul, ready to depart the next day, spoke to them and continued his message until midnight. 1 Corinthians 3:9-16 – For we are God's fellow workers; you are God's field, you are God's building. According to the grace of God which was given to me, as the wise* master builder I have laid the foundation, and another builds on it. But let each one take heed how he builds on it. For no other foundation can anyone lay than that which is laid, which is Jesus Christ. Now if anyone builds on this foundation with gold, silver, precious stones, wood, hay, straw, each one's work will become clear; for the Day will declare it, because it will be revealed by fire; and the fire will test each one's work, of what sort it is. If anyone's work which he has built on it endures, he will receive a reward. If anyone's work is burned, he will suffer loss; but he himself will be saved, yet so as through fire. Do you not know that you are a temple of God and that the Spirit of God dwells in you?

What is a church community? *1 Corinthians 14:26-31* – How is it then brethren? Whenever you come together, each of you has a psalm, has a teaching, has a tongue, has a revelation, has an interpretation. Let all things be done for edification. If anyone speaks in a tongue, let there be two or at the most three, each in turn, and let one interpret. But if there is no interpreter, let him keep silent in church, and let him speak to himself and to God. Let two or three prophets speak, and let the others judge. But if anything is revealed to another who sits by, let the first keep silent. For you can all prophesy one by one, that all may learn and all may be encouraged. And the spirits of the prophets are subject to the prophets. Seek spiritual gifts to edify the church and there must be order and balance in a church.

Ephesians 2:19-22 – Now, therefore, you are no longer strangers and foreigners, but fellow citizens with the saints and members of the household of God, having been built on the foundation of the apostles and prophets, Jesus Christ Himself being the chief cornerstone, in whom the whole building, being fitted together, grows into a holy temple in the Lord, in whom you also are being built together for a dwelling place of god in the Spirit.

What is a men's ministry? *Matthew 4:18-21* – And Jesus, walking by the Sea of Galilee, saw two brothers, Simon called Peter, and Andrew his brother, casting a net into the sea; for they were fishermen. Then He said to them, "Follow Me, and I will make you fishers of men." They immediately left their nets and followed Him. Going on from there, He saw two other brothers, James the son of Zebedee and John his brother, in the boat with Zebedee their father, mending their nets. He called to them, an immediately they left the boat and their father and followed Him. Discipleship. *2 Corinthians 5:17-20* – Therefore, if anyone is in Christ, he is a new creation; old things have passed away; behold, all

things have become new. Now all things are of God, who has reconciled us to Himself through Jesus Christ, and has given us the ministry of reconciliation, that is that God was in Christ reconciling the world to Himself, not imputing their trespasses to them and has committed to us the word of reconciliation. Now then, we are ambassadors for Christ, as though God were pleading through us: we implore you on Christ's behalf, be reconciled to God. Reconciliation.
Colossians 1:28 – Him we preach, warning every man and teaching every man in all wisdom, that we may present every man perfect in Christ Jesus. Instruction.
Hebrews 13:17 – Obey those who rule over you, and be submissive, for they watch out for your souls as those who must give account. Let them do so with joy and not with grief, for that would be unprofitable for you. Accountability.

Serve – Lead – Mentor – Pray – Teach – Train

We are a building under construction. It is the responsibility of our church leaders to be faithful to present the gospel of God. We, as ministers, are like contractors and we can only build how the boss wants us to, according to the blue prints. We not only have to have a relationship with Jesus, which is always important, but we must also be members of a living congregation. We are not islands! We can't just sit out in the ocean and be all by ourselves and wait for Jesus. Believers need each other for support.

His Spirit dwells within us as well as the entire body of Christ. Do nothing to tear down the body of God! If we do anything to one part of the body it affects the

whole body as the Spirit of God is in all of us. But build on the foundation of Jesus Christ. He is our cornerstone. *Matthew 21:42 – The stone that the builders rejected has become the chief cornerstone. This was the LORD's doing, and it is marvelous in our eyes. 1 Peter 2:4-6 – Coming to Him as to a living stone, rejected indeed by men, but chosen by God and precious, you also, as living stones, are being built up a spiritual house, a holy priesthood, to offer up spiritual sacrifices acceptable to God through Jesus Christ. Behold, I lay in Zion a chief cornerstone, elect, precious, and he who believes on Him will by no means be put to shame.*

Zion! What is it and how does it affect me? Zion is an actual place in Jerusalem. David conquered the Jebusites and is referred to as the city of David. He took the stronghold of Zion and built lived there. David built all around the city and reigned and ruled on Mount Zion or the City of David. (2 Samuel 5:6-9) King Solomon was instructed by God to build a temple to house the Ark of the Covenant and the Ark of the Covenant was removed from Mount Zion to its new home in Mount Moriah. (2 Chronicles 5:2)

Zion is also known as the place where the chosen ones will gather for refuge before the day of the Lord and His judgment. The remnants will return or the "left overs" from the group will come back, a small amount from the larger whole. And of course the "true church," the body of Christ. Jesus made it clear in *Matthew 7:14 – Because narrow is the gate and difficult is the way which leads to life, and there are few who find it.* Few compared to the many people who have lived in this world will find Zion in the last days. In *Isaiah 35:3-10* it describes what Zion will be like and who will be there!

He will save the weak and the sick, water shall burst forth in the wilderness, there will be a highway of holiness that the unclean cannot pass, only the redeemed or ransomed of the Lord shall return and there will be singing and joy, no sorrow. In *Psalms 125* Mount Zion is depicted as a symbol of security. In *Hebrews 12:18-24* Mount Zion is a place of countless blessings to all who are "registered" in heaven. *Revelations 14* Mount Zion is depicted as a symbol with the Lamb (Jesus) standing on top and with Him all the saints who have His Father's name written on their foreheads.

Chapter

13

Kingdom Man's Community Life

Church is where the kingdom man grows and matures, learns and worships. This is where we make connections with people like us, our support. This is where the Christians are, we are to seek and save the lost and those people are outside of the church! We need to fix the man problem in our country. The disease we have is not cancer, gout or intestinal problems. We can't blame politics or the newspaper. It comes down to men and what they do at home, at work, at church and in the community. *Malachi 4-6 – And he will turn the hearts of the fathers to the children, and the hearts of the children to their fathers, lest I come and strike the earth with a curse.* This is hope and healing for the men of the world. Jesus wants us all to turn and repent before the end of the earth and men are responsible for this. We are the leaders and supposed to make wise godly decisions. Instead we get lazy, but man goes first! We are the leaders. We need to lead our families, our churches and our communities. We have not been leading and so women have to do it and we LET THEM! Take the easy way out!

Ezra 7:9-10 – On the first day of the first month he began his journey from Babylon, and on the first day of the fifth month he came to Jerusalem, according to the good hand of his God upon him. For Ezra had prepared his heart to seek the Law of the LORD, and to do it, and to teach statutes and ordinances in Israel. The verses 9-28 show how Ezra taught the Law of the LORD. A true leader knows the way, goes the way and shows the way.

Successful leaders know how to love others. *1 Corinthians 8:1-3 – Now concerning things offered to idols; we know that we all have knowledge. Knowledge puffs up, but love edifies. And if anyone thinks that he knows anything, he knows nothing yet as he ought to know. But if anyone loves God, this one is known by Him.* Be willing to live by love. People we meet won't be Christian and they do things we don't approve of by our faith, but we love them the same. Paul said in *1 Corinthians 9:19-20 – for though I am free from all men, I have made myself a servant to all, that I might win the more; and to the Jews I became a Jew, that I might win Jews; to those who are under the law, as under the law, that I may win those who are under the law;* Not that Paul started hanging with the wrong crowd and doing what they do but he was sensitive to their traditions even though he did not follow them. That doesn't mean you can go to the bar and drink with them and then lead them to Jesus. Paul met them where they were but did not partake in their religion or he held back his beliefs so as to win them over.

The church has been set up to solve society's problems. There are three churches for every school but the people aren't in them. If people are in the churches they aren't doing anything productive to reach out. Society tries to solve problems with more funding, more programs, etc. The problem isn't solved out in society. The problems of the world are solved by kingdom men taking their place in the church, at home, at work, in the world and leading. Men banding together to fix our society and to bring our God back into it. How close are we to a Godless society in which we have to hide to worship him? That is a sad reality in many countries around the world and yet we deny it is happening in the United States. We are not allowed to teach or talk about God in school or say the pledge of allegiance because it mentions "one nation under God." However, we can talk about all the other gods or goddesses in the world! *Proverbs 29:2 – When the righteous are in authority, the people rejoice; but when a wicked man rules, the people groan.* Don't you think the United States is groaning? Our economy is sinking, gas prices are high, our dollar is worth less and our debt increases, we elect leaders into positions of authority that are ungodly, liars, cheaters.

Godly men stand up! Link arms with your neighbors, it's time to be men!

Reach the World!

Walking It and Living It

How to lead a Godley, purpose-filled life!

W e all need to know the meaning of life. Where should be going? What should we be doing? How do I discover my purpose? Do you feel like you are floating in the middle of the sea, unsure where the tide will take you? Everything we have talked about will guide you to a purpose filled life.

1. Men have to have a purpose. (work, church, family)

2. Men have to have someone to share it with. (spouse, best friend)

3. Men have to have a plan to accomplish numbers 1 & 2.

Let's find out what we should be doing by Paul's example. In the bible Paul is the most like us. He became saved after Jesus died and he had the WORST reputation around. When you saw Paul coming and you were a Christian, you had better run and hide because he was there to torture and kill followers of Christ. How many of us feel unworthy? True spirituality is growing in relationship, not following rules. We are destined to break rules and sin, but what happens when you have a relationship with someone? You don't want to hurt them, lie to them, etc. You will still break the rules because we all fall short and no one is perfect. But when you love someone, you WANT to be with them, you WANT to do things for them. Our relationship with Christ should emulate our marriage with our wives and vice versa (if you are married).

We have to have grace. Paul is constantly writing letters and visiting the churches he is over. They screw up, he instructs them and then encourages them. Grace allows us to move on. It is this period of grace that we are in that God has not sent Jesus back because he wills that none perish.

Faith. Faith means trust, we have to trust our wife and we have to trust our God. YES we have to do works for Jesus but we can't just do works and get to heaven. We will end up working so hard that we give up. We have all been given a measure of faith, just as we all have a measure of faith in our marriage. We can increase or decrease our faith. The more we see Jesus the more faith we will have, but how do we increase our faith? It is hard to trust in something that is not visible to the naked eye. If you walk and read His word, your faith will increase; it has to! The more we build relationship, the more we know our Daddy, the more we see through His eyes, the more our faith will grow. My wife depends on the wisdom of the Holy Spirit to tell her about everything. (Something I am trying to learn, although women are more in tune to the Spirit than men!) She can tell things about people as soon as she meets them, she can "feel" the temperature of a room, and she knows things without being told by a human. How? Godly wisdom! It is one of her gifting's that she is working on perfecting, foreknowledge. She wants to know what is going on in people's lives and receive words from the Lord to know how to speak to them and touch their lives. She is building her faith in God.

Paul shows us practicality and measurability. We can walk the walk and talk the talk by learning from him how to make a pathway to Jesus and disciple others to do the same. Remember true leaders have to show how to do it not just point the way and say do it. People need to see how someone else has been successful, especially when something seems impossible to achieve. Paul's book of Romans is a journey, as you will be able to see. He is travelling around, making disciples, building churches, and walking the walk! How many of us have become saved by the blood of Jesus and think, NOW WHAT? Great! I am going to heaven, WHAT ELSE DO I DO? HOW DO I DO IT? WHAT DOES HE WANT FROM ME?

The Book of Romans. Chapters 1 – 11 is considered theological or doctrine. Chapters 13 – 16 How to apply the doctrine to our daily lives. ***Romans 12:1*** – *I beseech you therefore, brethren, by the mercies of god, that you present your bodies a living sacrifice, holy, acceptable to God, which is your reasonable sacrifice.* Application of what Jesus taught us. What does reasonable mean? Logical. In other words, in light of all you have just learned what is the most logical thing to do? ***Romans 12:2*** – *Do not be conformed to the world, but be transformed by the renewing of the mind, that you may prove what is that good and acceptable and perfect will of God.* We live in a Godless society. Conform to the Word daily and use what we learn will prove or test the practice in everyday life. People need to know that God's will for us is good, acceptable and perfect.

HOW DO WE STAY ON THE PATH TO OUR PURPOSE?

Romans 12:3 – *For I say, through the grace given to me, to everyone who is among you, not to think of himself more highly than he ought to think, but to think soberly as God has dealt to each one a measure of faith.* Stay humble. All of us should remember the ONLY reason we have not been eliminated for our sins is JESUS. Grace, Grace, God's Grace. God is withholding judgment because Jesus makes intercession for us, be sober in that thought. God has given us all a measure of faith. Our faith keeps us going on the path to our purpose and every step of the way our faith will be tested and increased. We will have to rely on our faith more and more. God wants us to trust Him with our lives.

We are members of a body, the church. We all work differently or independently but function as one. ***Romans 12:4-8*** – *For as we have many members in one body, but all the members do not have the same function, so we, being many, are one body in Christ, and individually members of one another. Having then gifts differing according to the grace that is given to us, let us use them; if prophecy, let us prophesy in proportion to our faith; or ministry, let us use it in our ministering; he who teaches, in teaching; he who exhorts, in exhortation; he who gives, with liberality; he who leads with diligence; he who shows mercy, with cheerfulness.* We have gifts to share with others. It may be hidden under dirt and grime and the LORD reveals it or it may be very obvious to you and everyone around you. In whatever you have been given do it well!

Finally, behave like a Christian! *Romans 12:9-21 – Let love be without hypocrisy. Abhor what is evil. Cling to what is good. Be kindly affectionate to one another with brotherly love, in honor giving preference to one another; not lagging in diligence, fervent in spirit, serving the Lord; rejoicing in hope, patient in tribulation, continuing steadfastly in prayer; distributing to the needs of the saints, given to hospitality. Bless those who persecute you, bless and do not curse. Rejoice with those who rejoice, and weep with those who weep. Be of the same mind toward one another. Do not set your mind on high things, but associate with the humble. Do not be wise in your own opinion. Repay no one evil for evil. Have regard for good things in the sight of all men. If it is possible, as much as depends on you, live peaceably with all men. Beloved, do not avenge yourselves, but rather give place to wrath; for it is written, Vengeance is mine, I will repay, says the Lord. Therefore, if your enemy is hungry, feed him; If he is thirsty, give him a drink; For in so doing you will heap coals of fire on his head. Do not be overcome with evil, but overcome evil with good.* Difficult to chew? Difficult to walk? How do we accomplish this?

He has given us grace and a measure of faith.

What is the book of Romans about? God is righteous. God has delayed final redemption even though the believers suffer, He wills that none perish and all need Christ and salvation. Paul's purpose was to visit the Church of Rome. Paul shows order and logic as he presents the doctrine and theology of Jesus. Paul never met Jesus while he was alive. He met Jesus on the road to Damascus, while he was persecuting the church and killing Christians. *Acts 9:1-25 – v.4 "Saul, Saul, Why are you persecuting Me?" v.5 Saul says "Who are you Lord?" "I am Jesus, whom you are persecuting."* This is the church we have today, the disciples lived with Jesus in the flesh, Paul (then Saul) was converted after His death and resurrection just like you and I. Now not many will have that experience but we are alike in the fact, Paul was saved while being very ungodly and did not have the experience of knowing Jesus as a real man in the flesh.

Unfortunately our "religious" experiences may have left us hardened to relationship with Jesus. We see religious people misbehaving. We see people just going through the motions. We want to believe but don't have very many good examples. But we need people because not very many become saved by looking at nature. Even though the amazing world we live in should point to a creator, hardly anyone thinks that way. He made everything perfect and intricate, the human body is perfectly made, all the parts work together as one machine, God you are so amazing!! Most of us have to be led down a path to righteousness. People use God as the hammer coming down if you are bad, God is watching and He will see you and instilling fear! Who wants to have relationship with someone they fear. In Romans 12:1 Paul tells us that all God wants is us, offer our bodies as a living sacrifice. Don't look to other people to give us a good example on how to be a good Christian. They are just like us, imperfect. Look at our creator, who is perfect, who created us perfect but put us in a fallen world. God knows how to teach us how to behave and what our mission is. YES we need other Christians to fellowship and support each other. Let's face it, people who are unsaved think Christians are weird, different, crazy, etc., but people let us down and we have to remember they are just people trying to be godly just like you! Just keep believing, keep walking the path and take as many men with us as we can.